D1470000

Fascinating Food Chains

What Are Food Chains and Food Webs?

By Julia Vogel

Illustrated by Hazel Adams

Content Consultant
Jacques Finlay, PhD
Assistant Professor
Department of Ecology, Evolution, and Behavior
University of Minnesota

Published by Magic Wagon, a division of the ABDO Publishing Group, 8000 West 78th Street, Edina, Minnesota 55439. Copyright © 2011 by Abdo Consulting Group, Inc. International copyrights reserved in all countries. All rights reserved. No part of this book may be reproduced in any form without written permission from the publisher.

Looking Glass Library™ is a trademark and logo of Magic Wagon.

Printed in the United States of America, North Mankato, Minnesota.
042010
092010

Text by Julia Vogel
Illustrations by Hazel Adams
Edited by Nadia Higgins
Interior layout and design by Nicole Brecke
Cover design by Nicole Brecke

Library of Congress Cataloging-in-Publication Data
Vogel, Julia.
  What are food chains and food webs? / by Julia Vogel ; illustrated by Hazel Adams.
      p. cm. — (Fascinating food chains)
  Includes index.
  ISBN 978-1-60270-796-2
  1. Food chains (Ecology)—Juvenile literature. I. Adams, Hazel, 1983- ill. II. Title.
QH541.14.V64 2011
577'.16—dc22
                              2009051196

Table of Contents

Linked by Food Chains

A food chain tells who eats what. It shows how plants and animals need each other to survive and grow. Many food chains connected together create a food web.

A simple food chain can start with a sunflower plant. A mouse gobbles the plant's seeds. Then a black snake swallows the mouse. Later, a red-tailed hawk swoops down and eats the snake for dinner.

Food chains are in every corner of Earth. You can find them in the dry desert, the wet rain forest, and in the deep, dark ocean.

People are part of food chains, too. When we eat plants or animals, we are connected to all the living things on our planet.

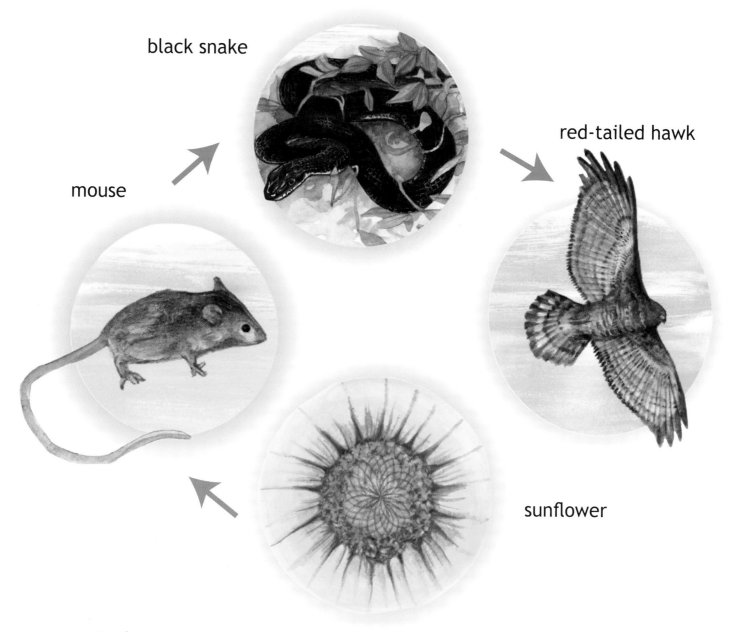

black snake

red-tailed hawk

mouse

sunflower

Food provides the energy and the nutrients that living things need to stay alive. The arrows show which way food's nutrients and energy move through a food chain.

Many Chains Make a Web

A mouse nibbles the sunflower's seed. Above, a caterpillar chews on the flower's leaves. Plants are often eaten by different animals.

Animals can eat a mix of foods, too. That mouse may also snatch corn from a garden. The corn in your garden may become your dinner—or a chicken's. Then the chicken may be eaten by a fox, or even you.

All this mixed-up eating means that plants and animals can be parts of many food chains. These connected chains are called food webs. You are part of a food web, too.

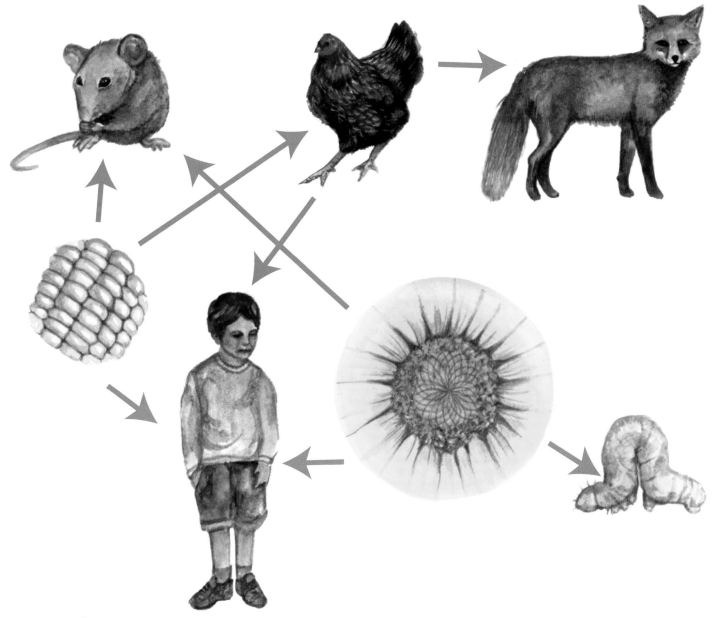

The arrows show the flow of nutrients and energy. For example, the mouse gets nutrients and energy from the corn and sunflower seeds it ate.

Plants Come First

A plant is the first link in a food chain. It doesn't eat other living things. But it still needs food. What does it do?

It makes its own food! A plant uses energy from sunlight, plus water and air, to make food. Nutrients in the soil also help it grow.

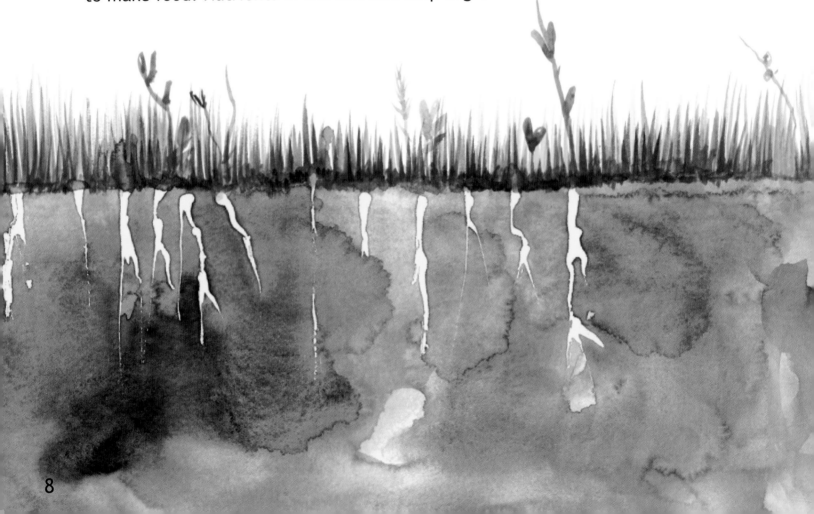

Down in the deep, dark ocean, some microbes can also make their own food. Instead of sunlight, energy from chemicals fuels these tiny life forms.

9

Herbivores Eat Plants

The plant uses some food to grow. It stores the rest in its leaves, stem, fruits, and seeds. Then along comes a plant eater, or herbivore. A rabbit nibbles on leaves. A deer chews an acorn. A butterfly sips nectar from a flower, or a bat gobbles fruit.

Energy and nutrients from the plants go into the herbivores' bodies. These animals are the next link in a food chain.

Herbivores can be as tiny as ants and as huge as elephants.

Carnivores Eat Meat

A black snake hides among the leaves, waiting. When a mouse scurries past, the snake strikes. The energy and nutrients the mouse got from sunflower seeds end up inside the snake.

The snake is a carnivore, or meat eater. Carnivores are the next link in the food chain.

The mouse needed energy to live and move. That means only some of the energy the mouse ate was left when it became food for the snake.

Predators and Prey

The snake is a predator. It hunts prey, such as the mouse. Many predators have special ways to catch and kill. Spiders spin sticky webs that trap passing flies. Starfish crack open shellfish with their strong arms.

Many prey animals have special ways of staying safe. Deer can run quickly from an enemy. Mice dig tunnels where they can hide.

A praying mantis looks like a green stick as it waits on a twig. The insect's prey doesn't notice it. That lets the mantis make a surprise attack.

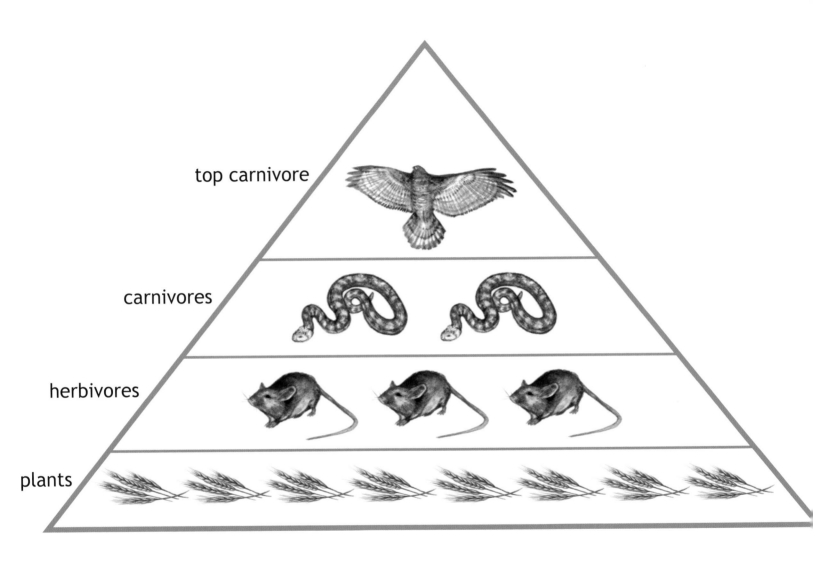

top carnivore

carnivores

herbivores

plants

There are more plants than animals in food chains. Animals get the energy they need from plants, but most energy is lost between each food chain link. That means there are fewer carnivores than herbivores and fewer animals than plants.

Top Carnivores Rule

A black snake swallows a mouse. The scaly creature is a carnivore. Then a red-tailed hawk drops down and grabs the snake. Energy and nutrients from the snake pass into the bird.

The hawk is a top carnivore. It eats other meat-eaters. Tigers and wolves are also top carnivores. These big, fierce animals are the top food chain link. Few other animals dare attack them.

Finding Enough to Eat

A red fox might eat wild grapes for lunch and a squirrel for dinner. This hungry animal is an omnivore. It eats both plants and animals.

Black bears, box turtles, and blue jays are also omnivores. Animals that eat only one kind of food might have trouble finding enough. But omnivores often find plenty to eat wherever they live.

By eating both plants and animals, omnivores link different food chains into food webs.

Whales, caribou, and many other animals travel far to find food. They connect food chains and webs around the world.

A deer may chew on leaves when the forest is green. But in the snowy winter, the animal makes do with twigs. Food chains change. Animals may have to find new things to eat.

Other animals travel to find food. In the north, cold winters kill most forest insects. So many of the birds that eat them fly south to warmer places.

Decomposers Clean Up

A fox will eat its fill of a dead bird. Then come earthworms, fungi, bacteria, and other tiny creatures. These decomposers feed on the leftovers. They break down dead animals, plants, and even animal waste. As they do, they recycle nutrients back into the soil. This helps plants grow.

As decomposers clean up, they're helping future food chains get off to a good start.

Imagine what the world would be like without decomposers! The ground would be covered in dead plants, animals, and animal waste.

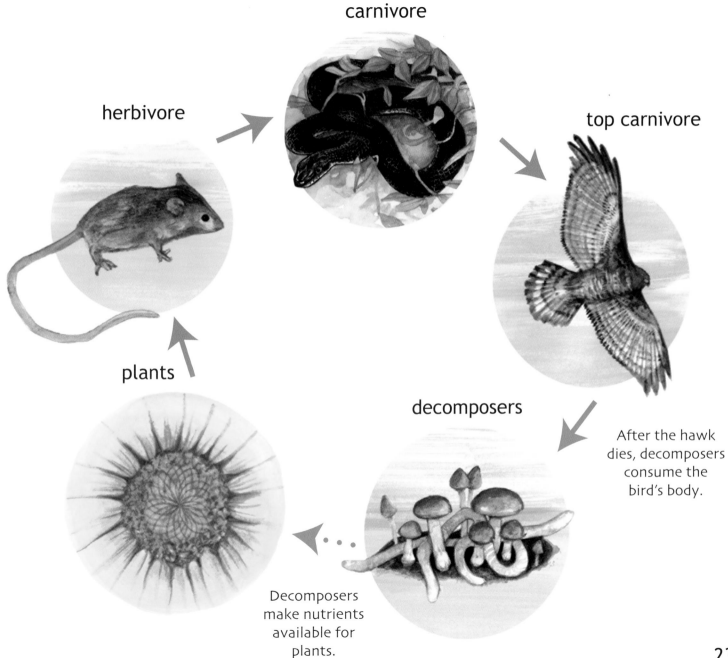

carnivore

herbivore

top carnivore

plants

decomposers

After the hawk dies, decomposers consume the bird's body.

Decomposers make nutrients available for plants.

People and the Food Chain

People eat hamburgers, fish, salad, and pie. We are omnivores in food chains.

Most people buy food at stores. The food was grown on farms. Farmers grow corn, wheat, apples, and many other plants. They keep cows for milk and chickens for eggs. They raise cattle, hogs, and other animals for meat.

Long ago, people did not buy much of their food from stores. They hunted and fished for meat. They gathered berries and nuts from wild forests.

25

Often, things people do to raise food end up hurting nature's food chains. People cut down forests or fill wetlands to make room for farms. Wildlife gets pushed out.

People also spray chemicals to kill insects that harm crops. But these sprays also kill helpful insects such as butterflies. What if a food chain link disappears? That could harm other creatures that depend on it.

More than 6.5 billion people live on Earth. We all need food and water to live, just like all the insects, birds, and other animals on the planet.

You can help protect food chains and food webs. One of the most fun ways is to plant a garden. When you plant your own tomatoes, you can grow them without chemicals.

Most important, keep learning about food chains and food webs. Tell others how important and interesting they are!

Living things need space. Protecting green places such as parks and wildlife areas is another way you can help food chains.

Food Chain Science

Scientists study food chains and food webs. They want to learn about all the ways plants and animals are connected.

In the past, people killed wild carnivores to protect farm animals. For example, hunters shot red-tailed hawks because they thought the birds killed farm chickens. But research showed the birds mostly eat mice and other small mammals. Farmers stopped shooting the hawks when they realized the birds were helping them by eating mice.

Hunters also shot wolves to protect elk, deer, and livestock. So many gray wolves were killed in the eastern United States that none survive there. Deer herds did grow—and grow! Eventually, there were so many deer and elk munching forest plants that some birds had trouble finding food and nesting spots.

In Yellowstone Park, scientists returned some wolves. The predators are hunting elk again, and the forests are growing back.

Scientific studies can help us understand predators' roles in food chains. Predators, like all wild animals, are important parts of food webs.

Fun Facts

Many people feed seeds, nuts, and other food to wild birds. Backyard bird feeding is one of the most popular hobbies in the United States.

Birds called red knots are world-traveling omnivores. They spend winter in South America. Then they fly to the Arctic to nest each summer. Their diet changes from snails and crabs in winter to seeds and flies in summer.

People from different places may eat very different things. You might think eating fried grasshoppers is odd, but a child from Thailand would think, "yum!"

People sometimes eat decomposers! Mushrooms help break down dead trees in the forest, but they also taste delicious on pizza.

Many animals change what they eat as they grow up. A lion cub drinks milk as a baby and eats zebra meat as an adult. A baby bluebird eats insect larvae but grows up to eat berries, seeds, and bugs.

Some animals are especially important to a food chain. For example, each spring horseshoe crabs lay billions of eggs on beaches along North America's East Coast. The eggs are important food for millions of red knots, turnstones, and other birds.

Some people choose not to eat meat. Instead, they eat fruits, grains, and lots of vegetables, so they are often called vegetarians.

Words to Know

bacteria - tiny living things that help break down dead plants and animals. Bacteria can only be seen with a microscope.

carnivore - an animal that eats another animal.

decomposers - tiny living things that live on the dead remains of plants and animals as well as animal waste.

energy - power needed to work or live.

herbivore - an animal that eats plants.

nutrients - chemicals that plants and animals need to live.

omnivore - an animal that eats plants and animals.

top carnivore - a carnivore that is not preyed on by other carnivores.

On the Web

To learn more about food chains and food webs, visit ABDO Group online at **www.abdopublishing.com**. Web sites about food chains and food webs are featured on our Book Links page. These links are routinely monitored and updated to provide the most current information available.

Index